To Gladys,
Keep the faith and your faith will keep you.
Rev.

When You Lack The Faith You Need

"Without faith it is impossible to please him..."

Hebrews 11:6

When You Lack the Faith You Need

Viable Solutions for Faith-Lapsing Moments

by

Tony A. Montgomery, Sr.

FOUR-G Publishers, Inc.
2005

When You Lack The Faith You Need

ISBN: 1885066-023

For copies of this book contact:

Rev. Tony A. Montgomery, Sr.
Missionary Union Baptist Church
1207 5th Avenue, North
Columbus, MS 39701
TEL: 662-352-6347
Email: REVMONTESR@AOL.COM

FOUR-G Publishers, Inc.
2101 Green Leaf Drive
Jonesboro, AR 72401
TEL: 870-934-0418

Cover Design by Kier Heyl

Printed in the UNITED STATES OF AMERICA

Contents

DEDICATION

Thanks, Grandma, for being my friend and
for teaching me to *"hold to God's unchanging hand."*

Marie Young Reed
1910-1997

INTRODUCTION

Faith is central to the Christian lifestyle. Faith is the guiding principle for possibility and opportunity, in spite of problems and obstacles. *"Faith honors God; God honors faith", someone once said. Scripture declares, "If you have faith as a grain of mustard seed, ye shall say unto this mountain, remove hence to yonder place; and it shall remove; and nothing shall be impossible unto you"* (Matthew 17:20). Scripture goes on to say, *"Without faith, it is impossible to please Him,..."* (Hebrews 11:6). It is the goal of every Christian to please God and, surely, when we come to mountains that impede our path to destiny, we want them moved.

But, be absolutely honest, have there been times in your life when you wanted to believe, but fear, distractions, waiting, a lack of resources and guidance kept you from believing? Do you believe in God, but sometimes have problems standing on His promises? Do you believe in God, but know your own limitations? Have you ever wondered how a Christian, a person of God, a church-going personality could be found low on faith? Well, let's face this one fact as Christians, persons of God, churchgoers, people who want to believe but struggle with believing, there are times in all our lives when we lack the faith that we need. We know what needs to be done. We know what God requires of us. We have heard the testimony of others. We have seen God's handywork. However, we still have these moments when we lack the faith that we need.

God knew that we would have these moments. Therefore, the word of God is littered with people who, just like you and me, have had these faith-lapsing moments. In these narratives, however, there are more than just problems; there are also viable solutions to faith-lapsing moments. Sometimes it's just a matter of waiting. Sometimes we have to get beyond fear. Sometimes we just have to allow God to be God, while we stand still and see our salvation.

In this book, hopefully, you will see yourself. Hopefully one of the characters or situations speaks to your personal situation. Hopefully, just as God made a way for them, you will learn to trust God to make a way for you. Just remember, in all of our lives, we all have times when we lack the faith that we need.

ACKNOWLEDGMENTS

I must start by thanking my best friend, my constant counselor, and personal attorney, my wife, Monique. Thanks for "believing in you and me." Thanks for all the encouragement in this endeavor. You were the first to read the book and the last. IBIYAM honey! To my kids, Sarah—my princess, Brooke—my angel, and T.J.—Minnie Me, you guys are our world. Mom and Dad, thanks for giving me every benefit of life, church, home, and school. Where would I be without you? You gave me life and modeled for me the Christian life style. Dad, thanks for all the lessons about preaching and pastoring. Mom, thanks for being there, and for the little talks when I couldn't get to Dad right away. What can I say to my siblings, Robert, Rushaleen, Gloria, Oneida, James (Billy), and Charles (Bobby)? You guys are the most sharing, caring, and giving brothers and sisters a little brother could have. If I am spoiled, it's your fault!

I have been blessed to be a part of four church congregations that were great, nurturing Christian environments—Second Mount Beulah Baptist, Temple Zion Baptist, St. Luke A.M.E., and the Antioch Baptist Church North.

Second Mount Beulah, I will never forget the love and caring shown by you during my father's pastorate. Temple Zion, I was 5 when Dad was called to pastor you, and 35 when he retired. Thanks for all the loving relationships, many that continue until this very day. Thanks for the power packed worship services. You guys know how to give God the praise. St. Luke, my grandmother's church, where I found the Lord and He saved my soul; there, I not only went to Sunday school, but was empowered to teach Sunday school. To Antioch Baptist Church North, where I learned the importance of serving the Lord, met my wife, was called by God, licensed, trained, ordained, and my girls were dedicated to the Lord, what a church!

Much thanks and appreciation to the Morehouse College family and faculty for helping me to break out of my shell. Special thanks to Debra Shumaker for the assistance, encouragement, and inspiration to finish what God has started. And last, but not least, love and appreciation to Missionary Union Baptist Church, the church I am blessed to pastor and call my family. Thanks for the inspiration and the love.

Whatever Shall We Do?

Part One

CHAPTER ONE

Trust The Savior

There are times in all our lives when we lack the faith that we need. These faith-lapsing occurrences, whether caused by situations or circumstances, happen to everyone. Faith lapses affect the not so well-to-do, and they also affect the well-to-do.

Tennis great, Serena Williams, illustrates one of these moments well. Sports fans and tennis fans alike recall Serena Williams prior to July 2002. Prominent? Yes. Powerful? Yes. A winner? Most times, unless she was facing her biggest challenge, big sister, Venus. As good and as promising an athlete as Serena is, whenever she and Venus would meet in head-to-head competition, she could never muster up the power and prowess she needed to defeat her big sister. She could be having a wonderful season, come into a tournament highly ranked, and still lose to Venus. It just seems that she lacked the faith that was needed when she needed it most. And that's how it is for us. We can be having a great year, doing well in school, climbing the ladder of success on the job, but when it's really time to perform, we are powerless. Our powerless performances are usually due to a lack of faith. But, as I mentioned earlier, Serena, in July 2002, finally found the faith that she needed, powered up, beat Venus, and has not looked back since. In fact, later that same year, she again overpowered her big sister in the biggest tennis venue in the world, Wimbledon.

There are times in all of our lives that we lack the faith we need.

What does that say to you and me, and people like Serena, who suffer from the same faith-lacking circumstances and situations? It says that, although we have a faith-lacking moment, it doesn't mean we are destined for failure. It does not mean that we will only know a life of losing. It does not mean that we will only know the agony of defeat and will never ascend to the thrill of victory.

How do I know? I know because you, Serena, and I have something in common with a biblical character that had this same problem, but he was able to overcome it and live victoriously. His name was Jairus. His occupation: ruler of the synagogue in Jerusalem. His situation or circumstance: a daughter was lying at the point of death, and then dying, while he was on his way home with "The Great Physician."

> *"And, behold, there cometh one of the rulers from the synagogue, Jairus by name; and when he saw him, he fell down at his feet, and besought him greatly, saying, My little daughter lieth at the point of death: I pray thee, come and lay thy hands on her, that she may be healed; and she shall live. And Jesus went with him; and much people followed him, and thronged him. While he yet spake, there came from the ruler of the synagogue's house certain which said, Thy daughter is dead; why troublest the Master any further?"*
>
> *(Mark 5:22-24; 35)*

What a situation. What a circumstance. He is a member of the church, a ruler in the church, but that has not stopped death from visiting his house. To make matters worse, he goes to the one physician he knows who specializes in handling this type of case, but, while he is on his way back home, his daughter dies. What a faith snatcher! What could be more troublesome to a believer than death in the midst of an exercise of faith? What could be more devastating to a parent than the death of a child?

And just like you and me, Jairus has his moment. I know because the text goes on to say that Jesus picks up on his faith-lacking moment.

> *"As soon as Jesus heard the word that was spoken, he saith unto the ruler of the synagogue, Be not afraid, only believe." (Mark 5:36)*

With those words of instruction and encouragement, Jairus obviously is able to get past his moment because the text goes on to chronicle for us how, instead of "tripping," he trusted Jesus to handle his situation.

> *"And he suffered no man to follow him, save Peter and James, and John, the brother of James. And he cometh to the house of the ruler of the synagogue, and seeth the tumult, and them that wept and wailed greatly. And when he was come in, he saith unto them, Why make ye this ado, and weep? the damsel is not dead, but sleepeth. And they laughed him to scorn. But when he had put them all out, he taketh the father and the mother of the damsel, and them that were with him, and entereth in where the damsel was lying. And he took the damsel by the hand, and said unto her, Talithacumi; which is, being interpreted, Damsel, I say unto thee, arise. And straightway the damsel arose, and walked; for she was of the age of twelve years. And they were astonished with a great astonishment. And he charged them straightly that no man should know it; and commanded that something should be given her to eat."*
>
> *(Mark 5:37-43)*

How did Jairus do it? How did he not lose his mind in this faith-lacking situation? O.K., I'll let you in on a secret. When Jairus' faith was lacking and failure was looming, he simply did not lose it, and Jesus fixed it!

Well, maybe you are saying to yourself, "That sounds good; tell me, how do I, like Jairus, overcome this kind of faith-lacking situation, and not lose it, so that Jesus can fix it?" Here's what you do. When you lack the faith that you need, *DON'T TRIP, TRUST THE SAVIOR!*

Don't Trip

To "trip," in slang terms, means to act in a manner that is not normally expected. It means to lose one's composure. It means to come unglued. It means to "go off," because the pressure of the situation is too much for you to handle. Chapter 5, verse 36, of the book of Mark records that Jesus said to Jairus, *"Don't be afraid."* Some other translations say, *"Fear not."* In the year 2003, we would say, *"Don't trip."*

When we lack the faith we need, most of us, Christians included, "trip." We act in a manner that is not normally expected. We lose our composure. We come unglued. We go off, because the pressure is too much for us to handle. I must illustrate. How about Abram and Sarai? Remember how they began to "trip" when the baby that God promised did not arrive when they thought he should have, and so they "tripped" really bad and decided to try to help God out? However, they ended up with two women in one house and a son Sarai later would despise. How about when Elijah received word that Jezebel had threatened his life for killing the prophets of Baal? Elijah ran in fear and, finally, sat under a juniper tree and "tripped," as he begged God to take his life. How about when Joshua and the children of Israel were defeated by the little city called Ai, and Joshua "tripped," fell down on the ground, and cried like a baby? Job's wife was fine as long as God was opening the windows of heaven and pouring them out blessings, but when God began to allow their possessions to be taken away, she began to "trip" and told Job, *"Curse God and die."* Didn't the disciples begin to "trip" on the boat in the midst of that violent storm out on the Sea of Galilee, although they had "the sea calmer" on board with them?

Can I ask you a question? How do you handle your faith-lacking situations? In fact, is there some situation that you are going through that has you about to "trip"?...about to cause you to act in a manner that is not normally expected?...about to cause you to lose your composure?...about to make you come unglued? Unfortunately, that's how you and I are at times. We "trip" too. But, can I ask you another question? What good does it do us to "trip"? Does "tripping" help make things better? Does "tripping" increase the balance in our bank accounts? Does "tripping" cause our circumstances to change? Does "tripping" make our families love us more? Does "tripping" set a good example for our children? Does "tripping" draw unsaved and unchurched persons to Christ?

Where has tripping gotten us?

So why do we "trip" then? I'll tell you why. We "trip" because we think that "tripping" will intimidate those whom we "trip" on. We "trip" because, in our minds, "tripping" helps us to vent our frustrations. We "trip" because we believe, in some far-fetched way, that "tripping" will change our circumstances.

But, honestly, where has "tripping" gotten us? "Tripping" has caused some father to lose his family. "Tripping" has caused some young person several days home from school, if not expulsion. "Tripping" has cost someone his/her integrity. "Tripping" has landed someone behind prison bars. "Tripping" has cost someone his/her job.

Isn't that the testimony that Bobby Knight's career leaves, as he had to exit in shame and blame as the head basketball coach at the University of Indiana? The man was a brilliant coach. He had coached some of the greatest players to ever touch a basketball. He is a living legend, and certainly will be a college basketball hall of famer. However, he will be forever remembered as the coach that yelled, screamed, threw chairs, and, on more than one occasion, was blamed for assaulting his players. In the final analysis, "tripping" cost Bobby Knight, and it costs you and me.

Can I suggest a better solution for us? Don't act in a manner that is not normally expected of a Christian. Don't lose it. Don't "trip." Instead, trust the Savior.

Trust The Savior

Mark 5: 36 records, after Jesus told Jairus not to "trip," he instructed Jairus, *"Only believe."* I like the way the Living Bible translates that text when it says Jesus told Jairus, *"Just trust me."* Trust means to take God at His word and rely on Him for salvation.

So, Jesus, who is God with us, was saying to Jairus, *"Take me at my word and rely on me for salvation."* Jesus knew that the news about Jairus' daughter was about to make him *trip* and become disbelieving in the possibility of deliverance, so he told Jairus, *"Disregard the bad news, take me at my word and rely on me for deliverance."* Jesus knew that the report from Jairus' house was about to cause him to act in a manner that was not consistent with that of a synagogue ruler, so Jesus told Jairus, *"Let me give you a report that has not been written but that I am about to send in to the Heavenly Headline news desk. Just trust me."*

Most of us would confess that we believe in the Jesus that advised Jairus, *"Just trust me."* But, we have some trouble allowing that same Jesus to give us a word, and relying on him for our salvation and deliverance. That is trust! Subsequently, that's why we fail. That's why we lose in this game called life. That's why we falter. That's why our churches aren't doing more to help usher in the kingdom on earth. That's why fathers are walking away from their families. That's why America goes to war instead of falling on its knees to pray. We believe in Jesus, but we don't trust Jesus! Can I ask you a question? What good does it do us to believe in a Savior, but then not trust him for deliverance?

This reminds me of a story that my wife and I read in a wonderful devotional for married couples called, "The Nightlight," by Dr. & Mrs. James Dobson. The story prods us to… *"Imagine you're near the beautiful but dangerous Niagara Falls. A circus performer has strung a rope across the falls with the intention of pushing a wheelbarrow from one side to the other. Just before stepping on the rope, he asks you, "Do you think that I can accomplish this feat?" His reputation has preceded him, so you reply that you believe he can walk the tightrope. In other words, you have faith that he will succeed. Then he says, "If you really believe I can do it, how about getting in the wheelbarrow and crossing with me?" Accepting his invitation would be an example of remarkable trust.*

When we lack the faith that we need, but we are still able to trust Jesus like Jairus trusted Jesus, we are getting into the wheelbarrow. We are moving beyond believing in Jesus healing someone else, and we are trusting him to heal us. We are pressing beyond Jesus quenching the thirst of the woman at the well, and we are picking up our own glass of living water.

So how about it? Can you not "trip," not lose it, and get into the wheelbarrow of trust while Jesus pushes you over your situation? That's trusting the Savior!

If we trust the Savior…

- He will deliver us, like he did Daniel, although we find ourselves in the lion dens of life.

- He will protect us as he did Shadrach, Meshach, and Abednego when they were thrown into a fiery furnace.

- He will provide for us just like he did for Abraham on a mountain of sacrifice.

- He will part our Red Seas, tumble our Jericho walls, and walk with us through the valley of the shadow of death.

Let me share a personal experience with you. It was the Friday before graduation at Morehouse College, my alma mater. We had been called together for final instructions as graduating seniors. Of course, we were given the usual do's and don'ts for Sunday's ceremony. Then we were given the final instructions to check the list posted on the glass of King International Chapel to see if our names were on the list for graduation. I knew that my name was there. I had finally achieved something great. I was a graduating senior from Morehouse College, where the minds of African American males are transformed. I had walked where King had walked. The philosophy of Mays and Thurman had challenged me. I was a graduating senior, at least until I went to the glass, went to the M's, and found no "Tony A. Montgomery." I found no Anthony T. Montgomery, a common transcription of my name since elementary school, by people who thought they knew more than my birth certificate about what my name was. In the words of my friend, Dr. Eric Mansfield, "My palms got sweaty, and my heart began to palpitate." How could this be? Why wasn't my name on the list? I gathered myself and said, "Self, don't start tripping. There is an explanation for this." I was then told to go to the registrar's office where I would be given an explanation.

I arrived at the registrar's office only to be told that I had not taken swimming. "Swimming," I said. "I took physical education before transferring from South Carolina State College." The registrar replied, "Maybe so, son, but you are required to take swimming to graduate. The only person that can do anything about this is the academic dean, Dean Jackson."

So, I immediately made my way to Dean Jackson's office, believing that all would soon be well. However, upon arrival at Dean Jackson's office, I was informed that he was out of the office until 3:00 p.m. So I made an appointment, and went over to the office where I had been gainfully employed since my sophomore year at Morehouse.

Back at the office, I sat watching the clock, hour after hour, believing that, once I talked to Dean Jackson, everything would be O.K. Well, 3:00 p.m. finally arrived. Of course, I was there early, at 2:30 p.m. Sure enough, at 3:00 p.m., Dean Jackson arrived and we sat down to review my transcripts. Dean Jackson looked over the records, as I told him my dilemma and assured him that I could swim. I said, "Dean, we can go to the pool right now, I will show you." After reviewing my records, Dean Jackson looked up at me, my eyes and ears clinging to his every word and gesture, as he said, "Son, everything is in order, congratulations. You have fulfilled all the requirements for graduation." I shook his hand in Morehouse fashion, thanked him for his time and help, and I walked across that stage a "Morehouse man."

I could have "tripped," but it would not have helped. It would not have been Christ-like. It would not have been Morehouse-like. It would not have been Montgomery-like. So, I trusted, not in my academic record, though it was in order; not in the list, because my name was not on it; not in my classmates, as they had already left me to begin their graduation festivities; not in the dean, though God used him to help me. I TRUSTED THE SAVIOR!

CHAPTER TWO

Be Patient

There is an old saying that suggests, "Time waits for no man," but, in this day and time, it could be said, "No man (nobody) likes to wait for time." In other words, the problem used to be that time would pass you by. However, the modern day problem is that time passes too slowly for most people. In this slow passage of time, most people tend to get impatient.

Nobody likes to wait for time.

Cipher, from the motion picture, "The Matrix," suffered from this impatient tendency. Cipher was a part of a team of rebels who were led by Morpheus, and their mission was to find this special person who would save the world from the Matrix. However, Cipher lacked patience. He was ready for the day when he could be free from their tiny craft. He longed for the day when he could be free from Morpheus' leadership. His freedom was, of course, tied to locating "The One," —this special individual. Day after day, year after year, person after person, they searched and looked for "The One." Needless to say, each one on the team was originally thought to possibly be "The One." Sadly, even after finding "The One," it seemed as though he was not all they had hoped he would be. Subsequently, Cipher's patience had worn thin, and so he devised a scheme to give over his team to the enemy, and to put an end to his waiting.

That's how it is when you lack faith in something or someone; it will cause you to become impatient. When impatience kicks in, look out, as anything can happen. It causes some to act prematurely. It causes others to act immaturely. It bids us to go off half-cocked. It places "ants in our pants."

You know I have a foundation for this proposition. In Genesis, chapter 15, verses 1-5, God promises Abram a son.

> *"After these things the word of the Lord came unto Abram in a vision, saying, Fear not, Abram: I am thy exceeding great reward. And Abram said, Lord God, what wilt thou give me, seeing I go childless, and the steward of my house is this Eliezer of Damascus? And Abram said, Behold, to me thou hast given no seed: and, lo, one born to my house is mine heir. And, behold, the word of the Lord came unto him, saying, This shalt not be thine heir; but he that shall come forth out of thine own bowels shall be thine heir. And he brought him forth abroad, and said, Look now toward*

heaven, and tell the stars, if thou be able to number them: and he said unto him, So shall thy seed be."
(Genesis 15:1-5)

However, just one chapter later, when the baby they were expecting and anticipating did not come as they thought he should, Abram and his wife, Sarai, showed a lack of faith and became impatient with God. They got antsy. They acted prematurely, and Sarai told Abram to take her handmaid, Hagar, and produce for them a son.

"Now Sarai Abram's wife bare him no children: and she had an handmaid, an Egyptian, whose name was Hagar. And Sarai said unto Abram, Behold now, the Lord hath restrained me from bearing: I pray thee, go in unto my handmaid; it may be that I may obtain children by her. And Abram hearkened to the voice of Sarai. And Abram's wife took Hagar her handmaid the Egyptian, after Abram had dwelt ten years in the land of Canaan, and gave her to her husband to be his wife. And he went in unto Hagar, and she conceived: and when she saw that she had conceived her mistress was despised in her eyes."
(Genesis 16:1-4)

From there it was a valley situation for Abram, Sarai, Hagar, and this newborn son, Ishmael. From there Abram and Sarai's impatience caused problems. Why? All because they lacked the faith they needed to wait on God.

But, not just Abram and Sarai, haven't we all fallen prey? Remember when you lacked faith in God to send you that someone special? Don't you remember how you looked for love in all the wrong places, and looked for love in too many faces? Or, how about when you lacked faith in God to open a door that was shut, and you impatiently walked off? No? How about when you lacked faith in God to increase your learning curve, so, instead of hanging in there and completing that course or finishing that degree, you gave up, and dropped the course that you still needed to graduate? Abram and Sarai lacked the faith they needed. You and I, at times, lack the faith we need. And when we lack the faith that we need, we become impatient with God.

When impatience kicks in, look out, anything can happen.

BUT, maybe you are saying, "Yes, but that's not what I want to do. That's not the way I want to handle faith-lacking situations. Is there another way? What are my options?"

Option 1: Hold Off

Well, first of all, when you lack the faith you need, hold off on deviating from God's plan. Don't go off on your own tangent. Don't edit the eternal road map.

Look with me to Genesis 15:1-4, and you will see that God promised Abram and Sarai a son. That was God's plan.

God's Plan

Abram (Father) + Sarai (Mother) = Isaac (Promised Seed)

However, as time passed, and the narrative unfolded to Genesis 16:1, Abram and Sarai's patience was getting the best of them, so they deviated from God's plan and devised their own plan.

Abram and Sarai's Plan

Abram (Father) + Hagar (Surrogate Mother) = Ishmael (Problem Seed)

Did you miss that? God had a perfect plan. Abram and Sarai thought they would help God out and offer their own plan. God knew what He was doing. Abram and Sarai could not wait on what God was doing, so they did their own thing. Let me make this plain, because we are so much like Abram and Sarai. Let's use the "By Friday" illustration to press my point. If God does not send us a mate *by Friday*, we will marry anybody who comes along on Saturday. If God does not supply us with the tuition we need for school *by Friday*, we will quit school altogether, and listen as Tom Joiner gives away thousands of dollars to needy students every Friday. If God does not deliver us from trouble *by Friday*, we will attempt to take on trouble all by ourselves, and get even deeper into trouble.

God does not have to do anything by Friday.

That's what happened to Abram and Sarai; they got into even deeper trouble. They went from not having a child to "Baby Mamma Drama." Trust me, waiting on the Lord in barrenness is better than "Baby Mamma Drama."

What Abram and Sarai should have done, and what we must do, is to hold off and be patient. The Bible does not promise that they who get antsy will get what they want. The Bible does not promise that they who get in a hurry will make things happen in a hurry. The Bible says, *"They that wait upon the Lord shall renew their strength, they shall mount up on wing as eagles, they shall run and not be weary, they shall walk and not faint."* So, don't get antsy. Don't get ahead of God. Don't deviate from God's plan. Hold off!

Option 2: Hold On

O.K., so you are holding off on deviating from God's plan! Well then, I better give you something to hold on to. Secondly, when you lack the faith you need, hold on to God's promises. Come with me to Genesis, chapter17. There, in Genesis 17, you will see God renewing his covenant with Abram, and reminding him of His promise to give him a son.

> *"As for me, behold, my covenant is with thee, and thou shalt be a father of many nations. Neither shall thy name any more be called Abram, but thy name shall be Abraham; for a father of many*

nations I made thee. And I will make thee exceeding fruitful, and I will make nations of thee, and kings shall come out of thee.' *(Genesis 17:4-7)*

In other words, God was saying to Abram, "Now here is the promise again; this time, hold on to it. This time, don't deviate from it. This time, don't do your own thing. This time, don't lean to your own understanding, but, in all your ways, acknowledge me, and I will direct your path." And, from then on, guess what? Abraham held on to the promise. Even when Sarah laughed, he held on to it. Although they both grew old and grey, he held on to it. Although the years rolled on, he held on to the promise.

Can I ask you a question? Are you holding on to God's promises? Maybe you are saying, "What promises?" God promises...

- *to supply our every need*, not according to the balance in our bank account, but according to His riches in glory.
- *joy*, although you may have cried all night long.
- *deliverance*, to the captive.
- *good measure*, to the liberal giver.
- *an eternal home*, to the believer.
- *sight,* to the blind.
- *healing,* to the sick.
- *comfort,* to the discomforted.

When you lack the faith you need and impatience is impending, HOLD ON to God's promises!

Option 3: Hold Tight

When you lack the faith you need, hold off on deviating from God's plan; hold on to God's promises. But, finally, and this is the be-all and end-all of the matter, hold tight, be patient, and God will provide!

Note, in Genesis, chapter 15, God promised. But, when we make our way to Genesis, chapter 21, God provided what He had promised, a son.

> *"And the Lord visited Sarah as He had said, and the Lord did unto Sarah as He had spoken. For Sarah conceived, and bare Abraham a son in his old age, at the set time of which God had spoken."*
> *(Genesis 21:1-2)*

Check it out:

- Chapter 15-Promise/Chapter 21-Provision.
- Chapter 15-Prayer/Chapter 21-Prayer Answered.
- Chapter 15-Need Presented/Chapter 21-Supply Provided.

What does the "/" represent? Hold tight! Be patient! Someone who is unknown, but not unwise, once said, *"Patience is the ability to keep your motor idling when you feel like stripping the gear!"*

In the next chapter, I will attempt to get away from stories from my college days, however, let me share one more story with you. It was, again, my senior year at Morehouse College. While the college is known for its academic excellence, ask anybody and they will tell you that the men at "The House" know how to throw a party. One such annual party was the infamous "Freak Nic," which began during my junior year. During my senior year the party grew to enormous proportions, and we had it at Washington Park that year. My "ace boon" in college, during my senior year, was Terry Johnson. Terry is a native of Atlanta, and a "Morehouse Man" through and through.

Be patient and God will provide.

Well, on the day of "Freak Nic" we were trailing one another, he in his VW Sirocco, I in my Audi 5000. As we turned on the street leading to the party at the park, we could see the party, but we were in bumper-to-bumper traffic that was delaying our arrival. Terry, being the native of Atlanta, told me to follow him because he knew a quicker, alternate route. So, we turned around and headed in another direction. As we proceeded along the alternate route, we soon arrived at the alternate entrance. However, at this entrance the pavement ended, and just beyond the pavement were railroad tracks. I said to Terry, "T, maybe this isn't such a good idea." But he gestured to me, "Man, I am not waiting in all that traffic." And so, while I sat idling my engine, Terry stripped the gears, and made his way over the railroad tracks. He almost made it, but his car's clearance over the rail was not high enough and, as he crossed the rail, the rail tore away his muffler. Well, needless to say, I decided to go back to the main entrance and, therefore, returned to the bumper-to-bumper traffic. When I arrived at the party, there was Terry already enjoying the party. But, while he was enjoying the party, his rush to get to the party was going to cost him. I, on the other hand, idled my engine, exercised some patience, and arrived at the same party, but with no bills after the party ended.

So, the next time you feel like stripping the gears when you need to idle your engine, think about Terry and me, and hold tight. Keep your motor idling, and trust God to provide what He promises!

CHAPTER THREE

Rest Assured

It is uncertainty, sometimes in who we are, and at times in what we are supposed to do, that causes a lack of faith to stop us dead in our tracks. These times of uncertainty manifest themselves in many different ways. Can I list some? When the doctor gives us a bad diagnosis. *Time of uncertainty.* When we have more month than money. *Time of uncertainty.* When trials seem too much to bear. *Time of uncertainty.* When our children go astray. *Time of uncertainty.* When our friends leave us high and dry. *Time of uncertainty.* When the company starts to downsize. *Time of uncertainty.* September 11 and post-September 11. *Times of uncertainty.*

However, when you walk with God in times of uncertainty, God will assure! God will *assure*? Yes, *assure* you. God, during times of discomfort, knows how to comfort. God, during times of hopelessness, knows how to give hope to the hopeless. God, during seasons of insecurity, knows how to give us security. God, during days of discouragement, knows how to encourage. God will assure you. Can I prove my proposition?

If you will come with me to Exodus, chapter 2, and read down through chapter 4, verse 18, you will encounter a man named Moses, who began his life in uncertainty.

> *"And the woman conceived, and bare a son: and when she saw him that he was a goodly child, she hid him three months. And when she could not longer hide him, she took for him an ark of bulrushes, and daubed it with slime and with pitch, and put the child therein; and she laid it in the flags by the river's brink. And his sister stood afar off, to wit what would be done with him. And the daughter of Pharaoh came down to wash herself at the river; and her maidens walked along by the river's side; and when she saw the ark among the flags, she sent her maid to fetch it."*
>
> (Exodus 2:2-5)

But, not only did he begin his life in uncertainty, uncertainty became a way of life.

> *"And it came to pass in those days, when Moses was grown, that he went out unto his brethren, and looked on their burdens: and he spied an Egyptian smiting a Hebrew, one of his brethren. And he looked this way and that way, and when he*

saw that there was no man, he slew the Egyptian, and hid him in the sand." (Exodus 2:11-12)

"Now when Pharaoh heard this thing, he sought to slay Moses. But Moses fled from the face of Pharaoh, and dwelt in the land of Midian: and he sat down by a well." (Exodus 2:15)

"Come now therefore, and I will send thee unto Pharaoh, that thou mayest bring forth my people the children of Israel out of Egypt. And Moses said unto God, Who am I, that I should go unto Pharaoh, and that I should bring forth the children of Israel out of Egypt. " (Exodus 3:10-11)

"And Moses said unto God, Behold, when I come unto the children of Israel, and shall say unto them, The God of your fathers hath sent me unto you; and they say to me, What is his name? what shall I say?" (Exodus 3:13)

"And Moses answered and said, But, behold, they will not believe me, nor harken unto my voice: for they shall say, The Lord hath not appeared unto thee. " (Exodus 4:1)

"And Moses said unto the Lord, O my Lord, I am not eloquent, neither heretofore, nor since thou hast spoken unto thy servant: but I am slow of speech, and of a slow tongue." (Exodus 4:10)

Of all the uncertainties, Exodus 3:10-11 is probably the greatest uncertainty. He is uncertain about who he is. He is uncertain about what he is supposed to do, and he is somewhat uncertain about who God is, and what God is able to do. In this moment of uncertainty, he begins to make excuses about his ability, about whether people will believe him, and about how he's supposed to explain all this to the people he is being sent to lead to salvation.

But watch God talk Moses from...

. . . doubt to faith.

. . . fear to courage.

. . . unbelief to belief.

. . . uncertainty to assurance!

How? I will tell you how. When uncertainty unnerves us and causes us to lack faith in ourselves and in God, at least God does two things:

He Provides Us With Profitable Experiences From Our Past

The life of Moses teaches us, first of all, that when we lack the faith we need, God assures us by providing profitable experiences from our past. Look back at chapters 2 and 3 of the book of Exodus. In chapter 2, you will see a number of profitable experiences from Moses' past. First of all, he grew up in Pharaoh's palace. There, in the palace, he learned the customs and culture of Egypt. There, in the palace, he hung out with Pharaoh. I know it has been said, "Know thyself." But it is just as important that we know our enemy. In the palace, he gained profitable knowledge about his future foe. But, most of all, while in the palace, he spent time watching the mistreatment of the Israelites under the hand of Pharaoh.

The God who created us and sustains us knows how to assure us.

Then, turn on over to chapter 3. In chapter 3 his profitable experiences continue, as he keeps the flock of his father-in-law, Jethro. Do you see the profitable experiences? He gains profitable leadership experience from keeping Jethro's flock, because soon he would be leading God's flock, Israel.

In the same manner, God provides profitable experiences from our past. David, the boy who would be king, also illustrates this powerful point in Samuel 17:34-37,when he says to King Saul...

> *"Your servant has been keeping his father's sheep,* when a *lion or a bear came and carried off a sheep from the flock, I went after it, struck it, and rescued the sheep from its mouth. When it turned on me, I seized it and killed it... The Lord who delivered me from the paw of the lion and the paw of the bear will deliver me from the hand of this Philistine."* (1 Samuel 17:34-37) NIV

Do you know why David said that with so much confidence and faith? David was drawing on a profitable experience from his past! He knew what God had done, so he knew what God could do. I know what you are saying, "I have not killed a lion or a bear, and I am not David." But, it does not really matter who you are, or what you have been through, God knows how to use what you have been through to take you to where you are going.

- So what, you used to hang out with a rough bunch...
- So what, you are from a single parent home...
- So what, you did not grow up with a silver spoon in your mouth...
- So what, you have not been in the church that long, and you know more about the streets than I do about the traditions of the church…
- So what, somebody dissed you, dogged you, and then dismissed you…

Guess what? IT'S PROFITABLE! It may have seemed it was going to kill you, but it's profitable. I know it may have seemed it was going to take you out, but now it's profitable. I know it seemed that it was going to ruin your reputation, but now it's profitable. I know you thought it was going to keep you from being somebody, but now it's profitable. I believe that Scripture says it this way,

"And we know that all things work together for the good to them that love God, to them who are called according to his purpose."
(Romans 8:28)

When you are uncertain and lack the faith you need, God will provide you with profitable experiences from your past, so that you can progress and prosper in your future.

He Supplies Us With Tools For Our Task

Not only does God provide profitable experiences from our past when we lack the faith we need, God assures us by supplying us with tools for our task. Moses was uncertain. He lacked faith. Here, in chapter 4 of the book of Exodus, Moses was going up against the strongest military power on the earth. He was going to deliver an oppressed people. So God, after hearing his excuses and noticing a lack of faith, supplied him with the tools for his task. What tools, you ask? In chapter 4, verse 2, God supplied him with a rod. In chapter 4, verses 6-9, God supplied him with the ability to work miracles and do wonders. In verse 10-16, God supplied him with his brother, Aaron, who would speak for him. In verse 17, God reminded him again to take the rod, *"where with thou shalt do signs."*

But God didn't just do that for Moses, God, over and over again, did the same for other biblical characters. God...

- grew the trees and told *Noah* the dimensions of the ark…

- shaped *Queen Esther* like a Coca-Cola bottle, and gave her the face of an angel, so that when the King of Persia saw her, he would say, *"My, my, my, my, my, my, you sure look good tonight"…*

- provided a jawbone and great strength for *Samson* to slay the Philistines…

- supplied *Elijah and Elisha* a cloak with which they could work great miracles....

Don't you know that God will also do that for you and me? In fact, He already has. Someone has the tool of encouragement to lift the lowest of spirits. Someone has the tool of companionship to be a friend that will stick closer than a brother. Someone has the tool of caregiving that allows them to provide tender loving care for an aging and ailing loved one. Someone has the tool of teaching and, when they teach, they know how to make it plain and apply truth to life.

I don't know what your tool is, but, if you have been brought to the point of uncertainty, just look in your toolbox, and you will see that God has supplied you with the tools for your task.

Rest Assured

When we are uncertain and lack the faith we need, God assures us by providing profitable experiences from our past. God assures us by supplying us with tools for our task. But, finally, Moses' life teaches us that, when you lack the faith that you need, rest assured, because, if God sends you, He will be with you! That's what He finally says to Moses,

"...Certainly, I will be with thee." (Exodus 3:12)

The word certainly means "sure to happen." So the sentence translates this way, *"Sure to happen, I will be with thee."* No, let me hip hop that, *"I am down with you, so you know it's on!"* It's like this, when you are sure that something is going to occur, there is no need to be whipped by worry. When you are sure something is going to happen, there is no need to walk the floor all night long. When you are sure, there is no need to look for excuses. When you are sure, there is no need to linger in the paralysis of analysis. When you are sure, there is no need to dodge your responsibility to do what you know is right. When you are sure, there is no need to avoid your date with destiny. When you are sure, there is no need to avoid God's will for your life.

My all time favorite Disney movie is "The Lion King." I liked it so much; my wife and I even saw it on Broadway. In the movie, after the untimely death of Cyba's father, Cyba is tricked by his uncle into running away from home and his ultimate destiny to be king of the lions. After some time, he bumps into an old childhood friend who challenges him to come back home and take his rightful place as king. Cyba, of course has many reasons why he can't return home, the biggest reason being the guilt that he feels about his father's death. Well, in a night vision, he is visited by his father who assures him that he is not to blame for his death, he needs to take his rightful place as king, and that he and all the past kings will be with him looking down from above. Well, of course you know, Cyba wasted no more time outside his destiny. He went back home, dealt with his uncle and took his rightful place as king.

Can I ask you a question? Are you avoiding your destiny? Rest assured, God will be with you. So go and take your rightful place.

CHAPTER FOUR

Distance Yourself From Distractions

Nothing messes with us like distractions. A distraction is something that is less important that pulls our minds from those things that are important. Distractions are those matters of no value that crop up and pop up, and try to replace matters of great value. Distractions are the stuff that draws us away from where we belong and re-routes us to places we have no business being. Distractions are untruthful words that struggle to replace the truth. Distractions are unrighteous actions that try to lure us away from righteous actions. Distractions are items that try to get the attention of a watchful eye, and turn it into a wandering, roving eye. Distractions are events that transpire and conspire to take our minds off the main event.

Marion Jones, a few years ago, while attempting to win five gold medals in Sydney, could not help but be distracted by the troubles of her husband, C.J. Hunter. You will recall that Marion was well on her way to winning those five gold medals when, just hours before one of her competitions, the news broke that C.J. had been accused of testing positive for using an illegal substance during his training for the Olympics. As Marion appeared, coming to her husband's side, her tear-filled eyes told the world that she was being distracted by the news. And, just as we all expected, the distraction showed up in her performance in her remaining events. While she still made history, her dream of five gold medals went out the window.

Nothing messes with us like distractions.

Why? Distractions and a lack of faith go hand in hand. When we lack the faith we need, distractions will pull us from where God has planted us. Can I show you? Look with me to Genesis 2:8, 16-17. In these verses God plants Adam and Eve.

> *"And the Lord God planted a garden eastward in Eden; and there He put the man whom He had formed."*
>
> *"And the Lord commanded the man saying, "Of every tree of the garden thou mayest freely eat: but of the tree of knowledge of good and evil, thou shalt not eat of it: for in the day that thou eatest thereof thou shalt surely die."*

But, as quickly as God planted them, the serpent and a lack of faith distracted them, and pulled them from the place where God planted them. Check out verses 1-6 of chapter 3, of the book of Genesis. Look at verse six in particular.

> *"And when the woman saw that the tree was good for food, and that it was pleasant to the eyes, and a tree to be desired to make one wise, she took of the fruit thereof, and did eat, and gave also unto her husband with her; and he did eat."*

I have to make you see this. God had planted them in righteousness; the serpent and a lack of faith distracted them to unrighteousness. God had planted them in a garden of Eden; the serpent and a lack of faith distracted them to a den of sin. God had planted them in a place of prosperity; the serpent and a lack of faith distracted them, and was about to cause them to be evicted to a place of poverty. How could this happen? Let me give you a crash course in "Distractology."

Distractions lead to disruption, disruption leads to destruction.

Distractions, which are not of God, distract us. In other words, they set us off-track. In our state of "off-trackness", we cannot do what God has created and called us to do. We are said to be in a state of disruption at this point. Disrupted, we are then thrown into a state of confusion, where we question right and become captivated by wrong. And, once we are captivated by wrong, destruction is our end. Recap: Distraction leads to disruption—disruption leads to destruction.

Can I ask you a question? Have you ever been there? Have you ever lacked the faith you needed, become distracted and, before you knew it, distraction became disruption, and disruption was leading to your destruction? Let me ask you another question. Did you know what to do? Let me make some suggestions.

Maintain Godly actions

First of all, when you lack the faith that you need, and distractions are trying to pull you from where God planted you, Genesis, chapter 2, verses 15-17, teaches us to maintain godly actions. Check it out for yourself. God commanded Adam as to what he should do and should not do. In other words, God spelled out godly actions that He simply expected Adam to maintain, even in His absence. But, as the story unfolds, Adam and Eve have a lapse in faith and get distracted by the serpent, and, before they know it, they are pulled from where God planted them.

Let's back up. God commanded them. A command from God is usually stated in two forms, things we should do and things we should not do. In this instance, God was saying to Adam, *"of every tree of the garden thou mayest freely eat* (do)*...but of the tree of knowledge of good and evil thou mayest not eat of it* (don't do that)..." If Adam and Eve had simply done and not done what God commanded, it would have helped them maintain godly actions. A command is simply, but powerfully, the word of God, the Bible, the Scriptures, the law, the statues, the truth, and the gospel. In moments when you lack the faith you need; and distractions are trying to pull you from where God planted you, all you have to do is maintain godly actions and keep God's command. Here's how it works. If you keep God's command, His commands...

- will be a lamp unto your feet, and a light unto our pathway.
- will be a lamp; and the law is light, and reproofs of instructions are the way of life.
- Jeremiah says, they are a <u>devouring flame</u>.
- Ezekiel says, they are a <u>life giving force</u>.
- Paul told the Romans, they are a <u>saving power</u>, and the Ephesians, they are a <u>defensive weapon</u>.

Distance Yourself From Distractions

First of all, maintain godly actions, but that's not all because, clearly, that's what Adam and Eve were engaging in when, all of a sudden, a distraction came along. So what do we do with the distraction? When you lack the faith you need and distractions are pulling you from where God planted you, do what Adam and Eve did not do, distance yourself from distractions.

Come with me to chapter 3, verses 1 through 6. There you

will see Adam and Eve being distracted by a scheming serpent. They get so distracted that they are pulled from where God planted them.

That's the same thing that happens to us from time to time. God plants us in marriages, relationships, positions of leadership, at peace with Him, and serving in ministries at the church. But that scheming serpent, Satan, knows how to distract us—doesn't he? He knows how to distract us with people and things that are distructive to our marriages and relationships. He knows how to distract us and cause us to abuse the power of our position. He knows how to distract us and throws things at us that disturb our peace with God. He knows how to distract us with worldly activities that take the place of kingdom activities. The problem is, before we know it, just like with Adam and Eve, the distraction pulls us from where God planted us.

Let me give you some biblical illustrations..

- Samson was planted as a "he-man," but he was constantly distracted by his "she-weakness."

- David was a great king, planted by God, but, one day on his balcony, he became distracted by Bathsheba's beauty.

- God was trying to get Lot and his family out of the den of sin, Sodom and Gomorrah, and plant them so He could prosper them, but Lot's wife got distracted while they were exiting, and was turned into a pillar of salt.

- Jesus was going to plant James and John in seats of their own, but they became distracted by someone else's seats. But Jesus quickly corrected them, and told them that the seats that had become such a distraction were already taken.

When distractions come, we can't just go wherever they lead us; we must run in other directions if we have to, and distance ourselves from them. When distractions whistle "yoo hoo" at us, we must cover our ears with our hands and distance ourselves from them. When people throw money at us to do what they want us to do, we must live in poverty, if it will put distance between ourselves and distractions.

Isn't that what Jesus did? No matter what happened or transpired in his life, he maintained godly actions and distanced himself from distractions. No matter what people said. No matter what people did to him. No matter what people or the devil offered him. No matter how green the grass looked on the other side of the fence. No matter what happened, he never let distractions get him off track. And so, instead of being conquered, he conquered. Instead of being a victim, he became a victor. Instead of dying a failure, he was faithful until death. Instead of being in the world and of the world, his life and death transformed the world.

CHAPTER FIVE

Follow Through

One of the hardest things to do is to follow through when things begin to fall through. Can I illustrate? You teach your children the dangers of drug addiction, but they still get strung out on drugs anyway. You put your time and energy into getting that promotion, and the promotion goes to someone who does not have the time, and is going to now use your energy to get their job done. You are giving your all to a job, sowing time and energy, but, instead of reaping a harvest, all you keep reaping is a barren field of nothing. You planned to be out of college in 4 years, however, you are now in the midst of your 5th year. Can you feel me now?

In one way or another, we have all experienced "falling through" situations and "falling through" circumstances. But, I wonder how many of us actually know how to handle these types of situations and circumstances. Well, in the Gospel of Matthew, I would like to introduce you to a brother named Joseph who knows how to handle falling through situations. Chapter 1, verses 18 through 25, chronicles the events leading up to the birth of Jesus of Nazareth. Preceding that noble event was the engagement and awaited marriage of his father, Joseph, and his mother, Mary. However, during the engagement, Scripture informs us,

> *"..before they came together, she was found with child of the Holy Ghost."* (Matthew 1:18)

There, in those few words, is a "falling through" situation. However, Scripture says that he didn't want to make a public spectacle of her, so he was going to divorce her privately. But, before carrying out his alternate plans, Joseph took some time to think things over. While he was thinking things over, the angel of the Lord appeared unto him and said,

> *"...Joseph, thou son of David, fear not to take unto thee Mary thy wife: for that which is conceived in her is of the Holy Ghost."* (Matthew 1:20)

Joseph, being the God-fearing man that he was, arose from his sleep and did just as the angel of the Lord had told him to do. That's what you and I have to learn to do when we face falling through situations. We must learn to do what God says to do, even when things don't go the way we planned. Let's take a closer look at Joseph's situation.

Remember, Things Will Not Always Go The Way We Planned

Well, when we look at Joseph's situation a little closer, we find that we must keep in mind that things will not always go the way we planned. As we look to verses 18 and 19, things are not going the way Joseph and Mary planned.

> *"...Now the birth of Jesus was on this wise: When as his mother Mary was espoused to Joseph, before they came together, she was found with child of the Holy Ghost. Then Joseph her husband, being a just man, and not willing to make her a public example, was minded to put her away privily."*
>
> (Matthew 1:18-19)

Joseph and Mary's wedding and marriage plans were probably no different, initially, than the average young couple—get married and then, when the Lord says so, have some kids. But THINGS were not the way they planned. They were not yet married, and Mary was already pregnant with a child that was not Joseph's.

But this was God's plan. Hopefully you do know, if this could happen to Joseph, surely it could happen to you. And it does. We plan. We calculate. We prepare. We ready ourselves. But, every now and then, stuff falls through or, for some reason or another, falls apart. When this happens your faith will be tested. Questions will plague your mind. Did I use the wrong type of glue?

Did the pieces just not fit together? Was our plan not practical? Could we have come up with a better plan? The answer is, "No." The only problem with your plan was that it was not God's plan. It was your plan, but not God's will. I hear you thinking. You are asking, "So, should I not plan because God is going to have His way?" No! Plan, but allow God to revise your plans. Plan, but allow God to change your plans. Plan, but leave room for the will of God. How do we do that?

Well, first of all, we must know what the will of God is. The Illustrated Dictionary of the Bible defines the will of God as the "wishing, desiring, or choosing of God." Secondly, what we must understand, as we remember that things will not always go the way we planned, is that the will of God is good and it is perfect.

> **Plan, but leave room for the will of God.**

That's not to say that the will of God is not difficult to achieve. That's not to say that the will of God is not difficult to live. That's not to say that the will of God is not difficult to accomplish. That's not to say that the will of God is not, at times, hard to understand. That's not to say that the will of God is not totally opposite of the way you would have planned your life. But one thing is for sure, the will of God is always good and perfect. We must learn to live in God's will.

Call A Time Out

But, not only do we learn that things don't always go the way we planned, Joseph also teaches us that, when things aren't going the way we planned, we should call a time-out and check things out. Look at Matthew 1:20.

> *"But while he thought on these things, behold, the angel of the Lord appeared unto him in a dream,..."* (Matthew 1:20)

Alexander Pope once said, "Fools rush in where angels fear to tread." Joseph knew what he wanted to do, and what he felt he needed to do, but he did not want to move too hastily. Joseph was no fool. He called a "time-out" so he could check things out.

That's what they do in sports when things are not going well; they call a time-out, so they can check things out. A time-out allows you to think things over and consider your options. A time-out gives the team a breather just before they go with any plan they may want to run.

A time-out allows you to think things over and consider your options.

Joseph was in the midst of a time-out in verse 20. He was checking things out and, sure enough, an angel came along and coached him in the midst of his time-out.

> *"...saying, Joseph, thou son of David, fear not to take unto thee Mary thy wife: for that which is conceived in her is of the Holy Ghost."*
> (Matthew 1:20)

The angel gave him just what he needed— instruction and encouragement. Can I ask you a question? Are you still running up and down the court of life, and things are not going the way you planned for them to go? Are you still running plays, but your plays aren't working? Well, before you go down to the divorce attorney; before you go down to the school to give the teacher a piece of your mind; before you quit your job; before you take things into your own hands; before you do something you might regret, you might need to call a time-out, so you can check things out!

Sometimes life moves so fast that the only way to see things clearly is to press pause on the DVD of life. In the motion picture *Minority Report,* starring Tom Cruise, this was the way they would solve crimes. Once the "pre-cogs" provided detailed images of a crime scene, they would study the still pictures until they could figure out what was going on, and what was going to happen. Time-outs in life do not literally stop time, no one can, but they make you feel that time has stopped long enough for you to talk to the coach of eternity and discern what's going on. For most of us, that's what we need in order to discern what's going on, a talk with the "Coach of Eternity."

Follow Through

Look back at Joseph's situation one more time, and there you will see the angel of the Lord give him this bit of instruction in verses 20-21.

> *"...behold, the angel of the Lord appeared unto him in a dream, saying, "Joseph, thou son of David, fear not to take unto Mary thy wife; for that which is conceived in her is of the Holy Ghost. And she shall bring forth a son, and thou shalt call his name JESUS: for he shall save his people from their sins."*

The angel was basically saying to Joseph, "All you have to do is follow through. All you have to do is trust God and walk by faith." Then look down to verses 24 and 25, where it says,

> *"Then Joseph being raised from sleep did as the angel of the Lord had bidden him, and took unto him his wife; and knew her not till she had brought forth her firstborn son; and he called his name JESUS."*

Joseph woke from his sleep and did just that; he followed through. He married Mary, although things seemed to be a mess. He walked the aisle, although earlier he wanted to walk away. He followed through, although things seemed to have fallen through.

When you lack the faith that you need, remember that things will not always go the way you planned. When things don't go the way you planned, call a time-out, so that you can check things out. But, after you have checked things out and they check out with the will of God, follow through.

My favorite basketball player of all time, "M.J.," Michael Jordan, illustrates this point. It was game 6 of the 1998 NBA finals, and the Chicago Bulls were playing the Utah Jazz. During the whole game, Michael had been coming up short on his jump shots. Well, with about eleven seconds left on the game clock, he stole the ball and brought it down the court. He had a lot of options, but Michael knew he was going to take the shot. If you watched the game, you will recall that most people thought that Michael was posing as he hit the game winning shot. But Michael said, "I consciously extended my hand up and out toward the target, because I had been coming up short. It looked like I was posing, but it was a fundamentally sound shot." The fundamental of which he spoke is called "follow through." As long as every shot has a follow through, that shot has the greatest chance of going in the basket. But, if there is no follow through, the shot has no chance of going in. It's the same way in life.

And, you will always come up short too, unless you follow through. This is not just tried and true of a jump shot in a basketball game, but it is tried and true when you are coming up short in the game of life. Try it. Extend your hand toward the will of God for your life and watch what happens. SWISH!!

CHAPTER SIX

Take Time To Be Sure

Image you are a lieutenant commander, on board a nuclear submarine, when radio communication problems prevent you from receiving your orders clearly enough for you to make a decision about whether you should fire on the Russians, and probably start World War III. To make matters worse, your ship's captain is a legend, and your uncertainty about firing on the Russians puts you at odds with him, and with most of the crew that is loyal to him. Well, if you are a movie buff like me, you know this is not imaginary, but it is fictional.

I have just described the opening scenes from the motion picture "Crimson Tide," starring Denzel Washington (Lt. Commander Ron Hunter) and Gene Hackman (Captain Frank Ramsey). "Crimson Tide" is an epic drama that depicts how to handle uncertainty in the face of a ticking clock. Uncertainty and a ticking clock? Isn't that the real problem with uncertainty? Who has time to be uncertain when a decision needs to be made? Well, if we carefully examine uncertainty according to the biblical character Gideon, we might conclude, "anyone who exercises the option to do so."

In the sixth chapter of the book of Judges, we are introduced to a young man named Gideon. Gideon was the son of Joash, a poor farmer. In chapter 6, God is calling him from farming to fighting for the Israelites against the Midianites, who were oppressing them. Now, while Gideon wants to do the Lord's will, he is uncertain about this calling and his own ability to carry it out. So, in order to be sure, he asked the Lord for some proof, some sign, some visible and tangible assurance of his mission. In verses 17-24, God assures Gideon of His faithfulness by consuming the flesh and the unleavened bread, and then, in verses 36-40, He assures Gideon by giving him another sign, dampening and then drying a fleece. The unique thing about the whole encounter was that God, the creator of the universe, was patient with Gideon and gave him the time he needed to be sure.

Kingdom business is not only achieved faithfully, but it is also achieved patiently.

Don't we all know and remember those times when we rushed to do something, and later were sorry we had indulged? Let me jog your memory. Someone knows the pain of rushing into a relationship that you were not sure you should be in. Remember the harm and the hurt you have caused by rushing to judge others.

You know how you destroyed the integrity of some co-worker by not checking him/her out for yourself, but, instead, you bought into the office gossip, and now you find yourself needing to quickly offer an apology. Why? All because you did not take the time to check things out!

As Christians, one of the great lessons we must learn is not to be in such a rush, and to take the time to be sure, because kingdom business is not only achieved faithfully, but it is also achieved patiently.

Take Time To Be Sure Of God

As we look into this biblical narrative about Gideon, first of all we learn that, when we are uncertain, we should take time to be sure of God's will for our lives. In verses 17-24, Gideon begins to check out God's will for his life. He has been told earlier by the angel of the Lord, *"The Lord is with you, you mighty man of valor!"* He has also been told, *"Go in this might of yours, and you shall save Israel from the hand of the Midianites."* The Lord, in verse 16, has also told Gideon, *"Surely I will be with you and you shall defeat the Midianites as one man."* So Gideon, in response to all of this, says in verse 17, *"If now I have found favor in Your sight, then show me a sign that it is You who walks with me."* In other words, Gideon wanted to be sure of God. And, in order for him to be sure, it was going to take a little time. Gideon needed time to go and cook some meat, and prepare bread that he would later present to the angel of the Lord. The angel of the Lord then miraculously consumed the meat and the unleavened bread as a sign, and Gideon then was convinced about the will of God for his life. Subsequently, when we check Gideon out after he is sure, and look down in verses 25-35, we see him beginning the work that God has called him to do in tearing down the altar of Baal, the false god that Israel has begun to worship in the place of God.

How many of us have gone out on a limb only to find out that God never called us out there?

Gideon, just like you and me, was essentially saying, "God, before I go out there on a limb, let me make sure that You told me to go." How many of us have gone out on a limb only to find out that God never called us out there? We went because we wanted to, not because we were sure of God. We went because Mamma said we should go, not because we were certain God was in it. We went because our friends said we should go, not because we knew God approved. We went because "so and so" went and it worked out for him. We went because we got tired of waiting for something to happen. Seldom have we gone out on a limb because we know God called us. And the only way to know for sure is to take time to be sure.

You need some biblical illustration, don't you?

- Moses stood on a mountain filibustering with God concerning His call to deliver Israel from Egypt, but, when he stopped filibustering, he was sure that God had called him, and nothing could stop him from the will of God; not a misunderstanding wife, an unwilling group of followers, and certainly not Pharoah.

- Jesus, knowing fully the plan of salvation, which included his suffering and death, took time to pray, not once, not twice, but three times. However, when he was sure, he left praying and said, "The hour is come."

So, take the time to make sure of God!!!

TAKE TIME TO BE SURE OF YOURSELF

Not only do we need to be sure of God and His will for our lives, part of the reason for Gideon's uncertainty was because he was not sure of himself. And so, in verses 36 through 40, Gideon is taking time to be sure of himself. He says to God, in verse 36, "*If you will save Israel by my hand, as you have said,...*" Can I translate that for you? Gideon was saying, "Hold up God, I am sure of You, now help me to be sure of myself." He knew what God was able to do. Now he needed assurance of his own abilities. Just as paralyzing as our lack of faith in God is our lack of faith in ourselves.

The hip-hop rapper, DMX, recorded a song entitled *"They Don't Know Who We Be."* But, many times when we are uncertain and lack the faith we need, the real problem is that *we don't know who we are*. Here it was, Gideon's very name meant "warrior," but based on his actions and/or inactions to this point, he did not seem to be aware of who he was in the eyes of God and those who had named him. That's how it is. Many times we have no idea of the power and potential God has granted us, and is willing to provide for those who are willing to take a stand for Him. We have no clue of the resources we have held hostage from within, all because of uncertainties. But, once we are sure of God and sure of ourselves, then we will...

The real problem is that we don't know who we are.

- like Moses, stop making excuses and become a legendary leader.

- like Shadrach, Meshach, and Abednego, refuse to bow down and worship idol gods, even if it means persecution.

- like Nehemiah, never leave our post, no matter how much trash the enemy talks.

- like Caleb, wholly follow the Lord, no matter what obstacles we may have to face, even mountains.

Are you unsure of your own abilities? Do you know what God can do, but lack faith in what you can do? TAKE TIME to be sure of yourself!!!

God Is Patient

Finally, the narrative on Gideon leaves us with one last powerful point. When we are uncertain, it's okay to take time to be sure, because God is patient.

Look back at Gideon's test that has now become his testimony. In verse 11, God called Gideon. In verse 17, he needed a little time and a sign to be sure of God. So God was patient, and gave Gideon some time and a sign. But, he was still not sure of himself. So, down in verse 36, Gideon says, "God, I am sure of You, but I now need to be sure of me. So could You give me a little more time and just one more sign?" God said, "Cool," and He made a fleece wet and the ground dry. However, Gideon still was not sure and said, "Lord, I know I am skating on thin ice, but could You please give me one more sign and just a little more time?" And you know what God did? God did not force Gideon to fight in uncertainty. God did not call Gideon a scaredy cat. God was patient! God gave him a little more time and another sign. He was patient with Gideon, and, when you are uncertain and lack the faith you need, He will be patient with you!

It's okay to take time to be sure.

Things That Only God Can Do

Part Two

CHAPTER SEVEN

The Lord Can Still Do Something

Sometimes things get so out of hand there seems to be no way to get a grip on them. Jan Schlichtmann, the flamboyant, lead attorney from the movie, "Civil Action," demonstrates this powerfully when a civil lawsuit that he files gets out of hand. The evidence is on his side, however, mounting bills from the suit begin to run Schlichtmann's firm out of business before the suit can be settled. Before the movie is over, the once high-powered attorney is abandoned by his partners, and most of his office equipment and assets have been repossessed. But, when it appears that there is nothing else that can be done, Jan sits at an old typewriter and composes a letter to the only entity that can help him and his clients, the Environmental Protection Agency. Subsequently, what seemed out of hand for him as an attorney, the Environmental Protection Agency was able to handle. This just goes to prove that, even when things get out of hand for us, there is always someone who can handle what we can't seem to get a grip on. Sometimes it's our health that gets out of hand. Sometimes its our children. Sometimes it's our finances that get out of hand. Sometimes it's relationships in our families that get out of hand. Sometimes it's our careers that get out of hand.

In the gospel of John, chapter 11, verses 1-27, is a similar situation. In this biblical narrative, Lazarus of Bethany, the brother of Mary and Martha, gets sick. The sisters, concerned for their brother and knowing Jesus' love for him, send for Jesus to come and see about him. But Jesus does not hurry to help, knowing that this is an opportunity to give glory to God, and to prove himself to be the son of God. He waits four days before he goes to give assistance. Of course, by the time he arrives, Lazarus is dead and buried. Nearing Bethany, Jesus is met by Martha, who says to him, "Lord, if you had been here my brother would not have died." Jesus, concerned because it appears that Martha's faith is lacking, and she does not realize who he is, says to her,

> *"I am the resurrection and the life: he who believes in me, though he may die, he shall live. And whoever lives and believes in me shall never die. Do you believe this?"* (John 11:25-26)

In other words, I can still do something! With Martha's faith renewed, she runs to get Mary. When Mary arrives in the place where Martha met Jesus, she echoes Martha and says,

"Lord, if you had been here my brother would not have died." (John 11:32)

Jesus, feeling her pain, realizing her agony and grief, groaned in the Spirit and was troubled. But, in spite of how out of hand things seemed, he says, "Where have you laid him?" Why? Because he knew he could still do something.

While this story reveals the lack of faith of the sisters, it also reveals the weakness in the faith of the disciples, who believe they have only come with Jesus to Bethany to die with him. Then there are the people of the town who question how Jesus could have let his friend die in the first place.

But, even though things seemed to be very out of hand, Jesus was not there to just weep over a deceased friend. Jesus was not there just to comfort grieving family members, but he was there because he knew he could still do something about their situation. He told them, "Take away the stone." He reminded Martha that, if she would believe, she would see the glory of God. He prayed to his Father. Then, in a loud voice, he cried out, "Lazarus come forth!" And you know what happened next, Lazarus, the one who had died, came forth! The question that may be crossing your mind, as it did mine, is, "Why does the Lord still do something when things get out of hand in our lives? When we lack the faith we need; when it seems that nothing else can be done; when we reach the end of our rope; when death dashes our hopes; when bereavement blinds our belief, why does the Lord still do something?

Specific Purpose For Our Situation

When things get out of hand in our lives, and we lack the faith we need, the Lord does something because he has a specific purpose for our situation. With Jesus, nothing just happens. There are no coincidences. Everything has a purpose, and so did Lazarus' death. John, chapter 11, records that Jesus said, in verse 4,

> *"This sickness is not unto death, but for the glory of God, that the son of God may be glorified through it."*

In verses 14 and 15 of the same chapter, Jesus tells the disciples,

> *"Lazarus is dead. And I am glad for your sakes that I was not there, that you may believe."*

Your question may now be, "Lord, do I have to go through bad things just so I can believe?" God's answer: "Yes, sometimes."

Did you know that faith grows when it's tested? It's like this. If you had never been down, how would you know that God could pick you up? If you had never been without resources, how would you know that God is a provider? If you had never been in a situation where you could not find your way, how would you know that God is a way maker? The songwriter says it this way, "Lord, if I never had a problem, how

With Jesus, nothing just happens.

would I know that you could solve them?" Sometimes, as we are going through life, when things are getting out of hand, we must realize that God may have a specific purpose for our situation.

Let me illustrate this. Remember in the movie, "An Officer and a Gentleman," how Lou Gossett is coming down hard on Richard Gere, who plays a Marine officer in training. He calls him names. He drills him hard and long. Lou tries to constantly create situations that drive Gere up the wall. It gets so bad and so out of hand, you start to realize that the situation is either going to make Gere or break Gere. Well, by the end of the movie, it becomes obvious that Lou was not trying to break him; he was, in fact, trying to make him into the officer the Marines wanted him to be. The training had purpose.

Well, whatever your situation is, God is not trying to break you. He has a specific purpose, and He's trying to make you into what He intends for you to be. To you it seems out of hand, but to God it's a part of the making and shaping process.

Let me give it to you like this. Abraham's situation of leaving Ur and going to Canaan was either going to make or break him. It was 1,000 miles, and he didn't even have a map, or a clue as to where he was going. God just said, "Go." It was going to make him or break him, but God's purpose was to elevate him and make him the father of a great nation. Moses had the same situation. Moses was set to lead Israel out of Egypt, and it was either going to make him or break him, but it was intended to make him a legendary leader and lawmaker. That's what God intended, and it did.

What I'm trying to say is, no matter what your situation, even if you lack the faith that is needed, God has a specific purpose. That's why He shows up. That's why He still does something. He's not going to let you down. He's not going to let you fall but so far. He's not going to let you sink but so low, before His purpose is revealed.

The Lord Is Sympathetic To Our Situation

The second thing that John, chapter 11, illustrates is that when things get out of hand and we lack the faith we need, the Lord does something about our situation, because he is sympathetic to our situation. In verses 32 though 36 of John 11, we see Jesus showing sympathy.

> *"Then, when Mary came where Jesus was, and saw Him, she fell down at his feet, saying to him, "Lord, if You had been here, my brother would not have died." Therefore, when Jesus saw her weeping, and the Jews who came with her weeping, he groaned in the spirit and was troubled. And he said, 'Where have you laid him?' They said to him, 'Lord, come and see.' Jesus wept. Then the Jews said, 'See how he loved him!'"*

Jesus arrived and, seeing Mary's tears and the tears of those following her, he wept. Why? Jesus was being sympathetic. Some people think that when you see someone is in trouble and you say,

"That sure is sad, God bless you," that they are being sympathetic. Not so. But, when someone sees someone else in need and then does something about that need, then they are being sympathetic.

Some people see our situations and they do nothing about them. When the Lord sees our situation and feels it, he does something about it. When we are sick, Jesus shows up and says about our sickness and our illness, "Just show me where it hurts." Even when you lack the faith that you need, even when you thought you would never get out of your sick bed, Jesus says, "Show me." When we mess up, Jesus says, "Show me where you messed up and I'll fix it." When your money gets low, Jesus says, "Show me what you have left. I'll do something about it. Show me that strained relationship with a family member; and I'll do something about it. Show me that failing ministry, you know, the one that you're supposed to be leading, but it is leading you. Show me, and I'll fix it."

He's The Only One Who Can

When you keep reading this text it becomes even more apparent why the Lord does something about our situations. You want to know why? Because he's the only one who can! Review the story again. Lazarus couldn't do anything, because he was dead. The disciples couldn't do anything because they were afraid and unbelieving. Martha couldn't do anything because she could only see the day of a future resurrection, although the resurrection and the life was standing in front of her. Mary couldn't do anything because she was grieving. Did you miss that? One more time, Lazarus was dead. The disciples were unbelieving and afraid. Martha could only see the day of the resurrection. Mary was suffering from a severe case of the "if thou hast been here." Who's left? The Lord!

When you lack the faith you need and things get out of hand, that's all you need. The Lord! Way Maker. The Lord! Heart Fixer. The Lord! Burden Bearer. Rock in a weary land! Lily in the Valley! The Lord! Bread when you are hungry! The Lord! Water when you are thirsty! The Lord! Doctor in a sick room and lawyer in a courtroom! He's the only one who can!

CHAPTER EIGHT

God Knows How To Sustain Us

Some situations and circumstances leave us wondering to ourselves, "How are we going to make it?" Maybe it's on your job, and you are wondering, "How am I going to make it?" Maybe it's a sensitive situation in your home, and you are wondering, "How am I going to make it?" Sickness, illness, problems, disease, chaos, are impacting the ones you love, and you are wondering, "How are we going to make it?" I don't know what your situation or circumstance may be, in particular, but in some way, shape, form, or fashion, life will make you wonder, "How am I going to make it?"

For those who are traveling, "How am I going to make the Boulevard?" Let me get straight to the point and tell you, you may not know how to sustain yourself, but God knows how to sustain you. God knows what it takes for you to "keep on keeping on." God knows what door to open for you that is perfect for you. He knows who you need in your life and when. He knows how much you need and how long you need it. And, if you just hang in there, God is going to do something for you that you have never seen Him do before.

How do I know? Because 1 Kings, chapter 17, verses 1 through 16, illustrates it. Elijah is the prophet from Tishbite of the inhabitants of Gilead. He is the one that stood before King Ahab and told him that it would not rain. Sure enough, it stopped raining. However, the stoppage of the rain caused a famine in Israel. The famine did not just affect Ahab, but it also affected all the people in Israel, including the prophet Elijah. But, God sustained him. How did He do it? God sent him to the Brook Cherith. There at the brook he drank water, and God sent ravens to take him *"bread and meat in the morning, and bread and meat in the evening; and he drank from the brook."*

But, as fate would have it, and God would allow it, the brook dried up and the ravens stopped feeding Elijah. So God said to Elijah, *"The brook is dried up, but I am not through sustaining you, so go over to Zarephath."* Zarephath was a city that lay 80 miles from the brook. Furthermore, being the way maker that He is, God told Elijah that, when he arrived in Zarephath, he would find a widow woman who would provide for him. So Elijah arrived there in Zarephath, and, sure enough, there was a widow woman gathering sticks. She was going into her house, and there, in the house, she planned to use her last handful of flour, and last little bit of oil in a jar, prepare it for herself and her son, and then she thought she was going to die.

But that was not in God's plans. God had planned to use this widow woman's last little bit to sustain Elijah, the widow woman, and her son. But, let's look at the woman's situation for a minute. She is a widow, which means that her husband is deceased. She has a son, which means that she is a single parent. And there is a famine going on, which has caused her to be down to her last little bit of flour and oil. Add all that up. It will make you wonder, "How is she going to make it?" How is this woman going to survive the famine? How is this woman going to survive with only a little bit of meal in a barrel and a little bit of oil in a cruse? How is she going to make it, not just by herself, but she also has a son who needs to survive, and a house guest? How is she going to make it? God is going to sustain her, that's how.

Don't forget, God sent Elijah there to sustain him. So, if God sent Elijah to her to be sustained, obviously God was going to sustain her in the process. And, honestly, that's how you and I make it. If you make it through life with all of its ups and downs, and ins and outs, don't pat yourself on the back. You did not sustain yourself. God sustained you. If you made it through some illness, some family crisis, some trial or tribulation, some financial short fall, some life threatening ordeal, it's because God sustained you. Maybe you are wondering, "How does God do it? How does He sustain us?"

Authoring Unimaginable Means

First, when we lack the faith we need, and wonder, "How are we going to make it?"—God sustains us by authoring unimaginable means. When we look at verse 12 of chapter 17, of the book of 1 Kings, the text says that the woman only had *"a hand of flour in a bin, and a little oil in a jar..."* That translates to unimaginable means. Let me define this. Unimaginable means unthinkable, unreasonable, irrational, or un-idealistic. Means is a way, a method, a procedure, or a system. Now let's put that together. In other words, God sustained the woman, her son, and Elijah by unthinkable methods, unreasonable procedures, and un-idealistic systems.

Where did this unimaginable means come from? God! God authored it. Don't you know? The reason why we lack the faith we need in the first place, and begin to wonder how we are going to make it, is because we can't imagine any means beyond what we are capable of making happen. That's why we can't sustain ourselves. At some point we become limited in imagination. Some people call it an inability to "think outside the box."

But God is not limited in imagination or means. With God there is no box. Let me illustrate this. It is unimaginable that God would use dust from the ground in the creative process of His crown in creation. But that's how God created man, from the dust of the ground. It is unimaginable that God would use the evil of Joseph's brothers, and the lies of Potiphar's wife to save Jacob, so that the nation of Israel

With God there is no box.

could be saved. It is unimaginable that God would put Namaan's healing in the muddy Jordan River, and not in the Abanah or the Pharpar Rivers of Damascus. It is unimaginable that God would take a persecutor like Saul and turn him into a powerful preacher and teacher like Paul. It is unimaginable that God would use ravens, scavenger birds that share food with no one, as a food share program with the prophet. It is unimaginable that God would send Elijah to a poor widow with dwindling resources to sustain him. But that's how God sustains us! He authors unimaginable means. Scripture says it this way, in Isaiah 55:9, *"For My (God) thoughts are not your thoughts, nor are your ways My (God) ways", says the Lord. For as the heavens are higher than the earth, so are My (God's) ways higher than your ways, and My (God's) thoughts than your thoughts."*

Shovels In Unending Measure

Secondly, when we wonder, "How are we going to make it?"— God sustains us by shoveling in unending measure. When you look at verse 14 of 1 Kings, chapter 17, God says that the unimaginable means that He is shoveling in, *"shall not be used up, nor ...run dry."* If you read on down to verse 16, the Bible says, *"The bin of flour was not used up, nor did the jar of oil run dry..."* Sure enough, they failed not, they wasted not, and they did not run out. Why? Because God was shoveling in unending measure.

I know that some college student can be a witness to this, because there have been times when your mother or father sent you some money and it ran out. It began to waste or fail. But you can also witness the fact that your grandma prayed up some unimaginable means from God, and they have been in unending measure well beyond college. Someone else can testify that the love of your life swept you off your feet, and said they would love you forever, but they left you for someone else, and said they weren't ever coming back. But, now that you have met Jesus, God is now authoring you unimaginable means, and sending you a soul mate whose love will be unending in measure. Someone else can testify that your life has been chaos and filled with calamity. But, in the midst of that, God has given you unimaginable means (peace) in unending measure (peace that passeth all understanding). So when you lack the faith that you need and wonder, "How am I going to make it?", remember God sustains us by authoring unimaginable means and by shoveling in unending measure!

Can I show you? God authored, in Luke 6:38, *"Give (unimaginable means), and it shall be given you; good measure, pressed down, shaken together, and running over shall men give unto your bosom (unending measure)!"* God authored, in John 3:16, *"For God so loved the world that He gave His only begotten son* (unimaginable means)*, that whosoever...*(unending measure)." And, maybe Thomas D. Chisholm penned it best,

"Great is Thy faithfulness! Great is Thy faithfulness!
Morning by morning, new mercies I see.
All that I have needed, Thy hand has provided.
Great is Thy faithfulness, Lord unto me!"

CHAPTER NINE

God Has A Word For You

In his insightful memoir, *A Way Out of No Way*, Andy Young recalls how the Civil Rights Movement was doing so well. Things were going the way they wanted them to go. Finally, the movement was on the move. They were getting national attention. They were getting support all over the country. Martin King had preached about the possibility of black people and white people living together in harmony. Martin had come and borne trials and tribulations, not just of African Americans as a people, but of the nation. He had come and anguished over the failures of the movement. Martin had come, like Jesus, giving sight to the blind of America. But, just as the movement was moving, just as the path was seemingly easier to walk in, on an April morning an assassin's bullet cut Martin King's life short. All of a sudden, Andy says, everything came to a grinding halt. All of a sudden, everything that they had been fighting for and struggling for seemed to fade into obscurity with Martin's death. Andy says that they were so down that they couldn't see their way. Andy recalled that Martin was their moral authority, but now he was gone. Martin King was tactical wisdom, but now he was gone. Martin King was the intellectual perspective for the movement, but now he was gone. Martin King was what appealed to the masses, but now he was gone. He was the one that everyone came to hear, but now he was gone. And there, in the absence of Martin, they sat and wondered, "What are we going to do now? Now that the dreamer is gone, how shall we continue the dream? Now that the King of Love is gone, how shall we love this nation that is trampling on us?" There they were, at their lowest point. They were down and they were about to be counted out. Their situation had gotten the best of them. The death of Martin King had dragged them into the valley of the shadow of death, and they were scared to death.

Have you ever been there, where your dreams are shattered? Have you ever been there, where something in life throws you down so hard you don't know if you will ever get up again? Have you ever been there, where life hit you so hard you wondered if you were going to survive the blow? One of the hardest things to do in life is to get up and go up after something knocks you down.

In the book of Joshua, chapter 1, we find a group of people who are down. They, like African Americans in the 1960's, had lost their leader, Moses. He had gone to the mountaintop and seen the promised land; however, he would not get there with them. The people began to weep and mourn the loss of their leader. For thirty days the Bible says they grieved. They wept until they could not weep any longer. But along came God and He saw them down and feeling hopeless. Moses' death had left them lacking the faith they needed to get up and move on. There they were on the banks of the Jordan, the promised land was just on the other side of the river, but they were stuck in sorrow. They were not standing, they were sitting, weeping, and grieving. But God came where they were with a word for a down people, in verses 2 through 9.

> *"Moses My servant is dead. Now therefore, arise, go over this Jordan, you and all this people, to the land which I am giving to them—them the children of Israel. Every place that the sole of your foot will tread upon I have given you, as I said to Moses. No man shall be able to stand before you all the days of your life; as I was with Moses, so I will be with you. I will not leave you nor forsake you. Be strong and of good courage,...Only be strong and very courageous,...Be strong and of good courage; do not be afraid, nor dismayed, for the Lord your God is with you wherever you go."*

God, even when Israel and Joshua lacked the faith they needed to move on, had a word for them. Are you feeling down? Are you in a low spot in life? Are you going through a valley situation? Well, God has a word for you too.

An Encouraging Word

First of all, when you are feeling down, God has an encouraging word. When we take a close look at Joshua, chapter 1, verses 2, 3, 5-7, and 9, the words that God speaks to Joshua are encouraging words. Here they were hopeless and without courage to journey on. Here they were low in spirit, and slow to take steps toward their destiny as a people. But God spoke encouraging words to them. To encourage means to instill with courage and hope. Notice that God did not say a word about what they couldn't do. God simply talked to Joshua about what he could do. God's words are intended to instill courage where there is cowardice. God's words are intended to instill hope where there is hopelessness. Sometimes that's all we need to get back on track. Sometimes that's all we need to get up from our down situations.

There is a set of twin boys in my family, James E. and Charles E. Montgomery. We affectionately call them Billy and Bobby. They have served as role models and mentors in my life. As a young man growing up, and even to this very day, they often call me and give me an encouraging word. They always know what to say. They always say what I need to hear to feel better. Their words always give me hope. Their words always cause me to work harder. Their words always give me courage to face life's trials.

To encourage means to instill with courage and hope.

And that's how it is with the Word of God. God's Word always says exactly what we need to hear. God's Word always says to us exactly what needs to be said. God's Word always encourages us to work harder to reach our goals. God's Word always leaves us with so much hope, no matter what the situation is.

Look with me at some encouraging words from God. Remember when Abraham was scared because things were not going the way that he wanted them to, and God spoke to him saying, *"Fear not, Abram, I am thy shield, and thy exceeding great reward."* (Genesis 15:1) Then there was Isaiah who was not certain that he would make it through a rough time, but God spoke to him saying, *"For I the Lord thy God will hold thy right hand, saying unto thee, 'Fear not: I will help thee.'"* (Isaiah 41:13) Just like God encouraged Joshua, Israel, and the saints before us with His words, when we lack the faith we need and are feeling down, God has an encouraging word for us.

An Inspiring Word

But, not only do God's words encourage us when we lack the faith that we need and we are feeling down, but, if you look a little further to Joshua 1:10, you will see that God's word is an inspiring word. The verse says,

> *"Then Joshua commanded the officers of the people,..."*

Here was a man who was down and out, grieving, and not moving toward his destiny. Here was a leader who was not moving people on to God's agenda, as Henry Blackaby, the author of *Spiritual Leadership,* suggests spiritual leaders ought to do. However, after God spoke to him he was inspired. To be inspired simply means to be influenced, to move, or to guide something or someone. Look at this closely,

— God's word <u>influenced</u> Joshua in vs. 1-9, *Then, Joshua commanded the officers of the people,*

— God's word <u>guided</u>...*Then, Joshua commanded the officers of the people,*

— God's word <u>moved</u>...*Then, Joshua commanded the officers of the people,*

God had a word for Joshua that inspired him! Can I ask you a question? If God would do that for Joshua, don't you think that He has a word that will inspire you and me?

To be inspired simply means to be influenced, to move, or to guide something or someone.

When the world tells us that we can't, and it gets us down and out, we must remember the Word of God has a word for can't situations... *"I can do all things through Christ."* (Philippians 4:13) When we are caught between our enemies and some obstacle that seems impassable, and get depressed and distraught, we must remember God's word says,

"Fear not, stand still and see the salvation of the Lord." (Exodus 14:13) When we lack the faith that we need because some situation has gotten us down, God has a word for us that is encouraging and inspiring.

I must illustrate this. The February 1999 edition of Reader's Digest had an article entitled, "The Transformation of Robin Williams." In that article, Robin Williams shared a time when he was down and out. His life, he said, was spiraling out of control. His wife was pregnant. His friend, John Belushi, had died of a drug overdose. In the midst of all this his father became ill. One afternoon he went to pay a visit to his ailing father. As they discussed Robin's doubts, and his dreams for the future, his father shared with him the story of why he decided to get out of the automotive business. He said, "The automobile industry was going downhill, and I loved what I did, but all they wanted to do was churn out as many cars as they could. The companies were losing their sense of pride in their product. I couldn't stand by and watch it happen; I had to get out." "Robin," the article said, "knew that he, too, had to take some risks and reclaim the life he wanted." Subsequently, inspired by his father's words, Robin took some risks and reclaimed control of his life.

Are you feeling down? Does it seem that your life is spiraling out of control? Well, just like with Robin Williams, your Father, your Heavenly Father has a word for you.

Are you suffering? Romans 8:18 says, *"For I reckon that the sufferings of this present time are not worthy to be compared with the glory which shall be revealed in us."* Do you find yourself crying in the midnight hour? Psalm 30:5 says, "*Weeping endures for a night, but joy cometh in the morning.*" Are you tired of doing "good," but not seeing the fruit of your activity? Galatians 6:9 says, "*Let us not be weary in well doing; for in due season we shall reap, if we faint not.*" Are the demands on your pockets greater than the supply in the bank account? Philippians 4:19 says, "*And my God shall supply all your needs according to His riches, in glory by Christ Jesus.*" Is life in general about to make you lose your mind? Philippians 4:18 says, "*Finally brethren, whatsoever things are true...honest...just...pure...lovely...of good report, if there be any virtue, and if there be any praise, think on these things.*"

Whatever your situation may be; whatever has you feeling down; God has an encouraging and inspiring word for you! Have you read your Bible lately?

CHAPTER TEN

The Lord Will Help You With Your Unbelief

Have you ever tried to believe, ended up at a point of unbelief, and then said, "Now what?" Unbelief is a lack of faith in God and His provisions, and we all suffer from it from time to time. As strange as that may seem, it happens. It happens when you pay your tithes instead of your light bill and your lights get turned off. It happens when you pray for God to heal your loved ones, and they die anyway, in spite of all your prayers. It happens when you pray, then go to the bank and the bank denies you a loan, despite what you ask God for. It happens when you train your children in the way they should go, teaching them about the Lord, giving them every benefit of home, church, and school, but you stay at the jail house year after year. Now all you can say is, "Now what? I tried to believe. I tried to have faith. I tried to have the courage of David, and the fortitude of the Hebrew boys. I tried to trust in the Lord and lean not to my own understanding, but here I am again at unbelief. Now what?" Can a Christian get some help? Sure you can.

The father of the demon possessed boy in Mark, chapter 9, was helped. There he was, surrounded by the disciples, who were surrounded by the scribes, who were surrounded by a multitude, trying to believe, but falling short. The problem is anything short of belief is unbelief. But, look closely, because, in spite of the unbelief and disarray, Jesus arrived on the scene. Upon his arrival, he immediately asked what was happening. The father spoke up and said,

> *"I brought my son, who has a mute spirit. And wherever it seizes him, it throws him down; he foams at the mouth, gnashes his teeth, and becomes rigid. So I spoke to your disciples that they should cast it out, but they could not."*

Of course, if you keep on reading, Jesus has some choice words for this situation. After those choice words, he shows his concern and says to the father, *"Bring him to me."* He then stretches his concern farther to inquire, "How long has this been going on?" The father answers him and pleads with him, *"If you can do anything, have compassion on us and help us."* Jesus senses this father's frustrations and lack of faith and replies, *"If you can believe, all things are possible to him who believes."* This father, struggling to believe, facing unbelief, cries with tears and says, *"Lord, I believe; help my unbelief!"*

Can you feel this father's pain? *"Lord, I believe; help my unbelief!"* Have you ever experienced that kind of pain and said, "Lord, I want to be committed; help my lack of commitment! Lord, I want to be more patient; help my impatience! Lord, I want to be more supportive; help my inability to be supportive!"

So, what does Jesus do for the father who is in need of some help? He cast the deaf and dumb spirit out of the boy, and gave the father and all gathered around him a reason to believe. That's what the Lord will do to help you with your unbelief. He will not leave you at a point of unbelief. He will not allow you to go out on a limb in search of faith, and then allow you to fall. Jesus will help you with your unbelief! Did you miss it? Let me show it to you in slow motion.

Shows Up In Spite of Our Unbelief

Look back at verses 14 and 15 of Mark, chapter 9. There you will see unbelieving disciples, an unbelieving multitude, and some unbelieving and disputing scribes. But that's also where you will see Jesus show up. Verse 14 says, *"And when he came to the disciples,..."* In verse 15, Mark records that the people were amazed at his arrival and ran to greet him. Here is all this unbelief in one location, but Jesus showed up there.

Can I let you in on a secret? Jesus is not afraid to show up anywhere or at anytime. Hip-Hoppers from "Generation Next" would say, "He ain't never scared." But this isn't the first time that he has done this. Remember after the resurrection, when he appeared to the disciples, but Thomas was absent and, therefore, left doubting? In spite of doubt, Jesus showed up. In fact, he walked in with *"the doors being shut."* He showed up on the road to Emmaus to two doubting and disheartened disciples. He showed up at the grave of Lazarus, after dealing with his grieving and doubting sisters who thought that there was nothing else that could be done. Doubt is not kryptonite for Jesus. Therefore, he will still show up in spite of your unbelief!

Jesus is not afraid to show up anywhere or anytime.

The Lord Shows Concern About Our Unbelief

But, you know what? When you are at a point of unbelief, another bystander does not mean much—does he? Well, I want you to know that when Jesus shows up at your point of unbelief, he is not there as a spectator. He shows concern about our unbelief. In verses 16 through 23 of Mark, chapter 9, we see that Jesus jumped right in with both feet and began to inquire about what was happening. After being told, and telling some folk off, he then proceeded to examine his new patient a little closer. He began to ask specific questions about the boy's condition like, "How long has this been happening?" After sensing that a little more doubt had crept into the situation from the boy's father, Jesus gave a prognosis concerning the boy's situation and said, *"If you can believe, all things are possible to him who believes."*

Bystanders stand by, but Jesus shows concern. Onlookers look on, but Jesus takes a closer look. Passersby pass by, but Jesus stops by and shows concern for our unbelief.

Bystanders stand by, but Jesus shows concern.

Do you know what happens when someone shows concern about what you are going through? Your burden begins to get a little lighter, when you know someone is concerned about what's happening in your life. You start to feel as though maybe there is some hope for your hopeless situation, when someone shows concern about your circumstances.

JESUS GIVES US A REASON TO BELIEVE

So now, Jesus showed up and showed concern about what was going on with this father and his son. Then what? Well, the poor father, after hearing the prognosis, and struggling between enough faith to seek Jesus and not enough faith to believe Jesus, cried out with tears, *"Lord, I believe; help my unbelief."*

Can I ask you a question? Have you, like this father, cried out? Have you cried out with tears? Have you poured out your heart to the *Heart Fixer*? Have you emptied the thoughts of your mind to the *Mind Regulator*? Hebrews 4:15 reminds us,

> *"For we do not have a high priest who can not sympathize with our weaknesses, but in all points was tempted as we are, yet without sin. Let us come boldly to the throne of grace, that we may obtain mercy and find grace to help in the time of need."*

Have you cried out, *"Lord, I believe, help me with my unbelief"?* I can't let you miss this. There is always something that God expects us to do, as it relates to faith and a lack of faith. The father did that. He came asking, seeking, and knocking. He brought his son to get him the help he so desperately needed. However, there is some stuff that only Jesus can do as it relates to faith. Jesus, in verse 25, did something to help the father, the disciples, the multitude, and the scribes to believe; he rebuked that unclean spirit out of the boy forever! He helped them with their unbelief! Another sermon was not going to get the point across. Another bible study was not going to make things clearer. A song was not going to soothe the anguish of his dilemma. The father needed help, not just with his son, but with his faith, and Jesus helped him to believe by healing his son!

When you are struggling to believe (lack the faith you need) and, in trying to believe, end up at unbelief, Jesus will show up in spite of your unbelief, show concern about your unbelief, and GIVE YOU A REASON TO BELIEVE! That's what he did for the disciples and Thomas in the upper room. That's what he did for those two disciples on the road to Emmaus. That's what he did for the woman at the well. That's what he did for Zaccheus, who was up a tree and out on a limb. In the words of the hymn writer and the Seasoned Saints, *"There is no secret, what God can do. What He has done for others, He will do for you!"*

FINAL NOTE

God Will Strengthen You

We have peeped into the portfolios of many of the faith tested heroes of the Bible. However, I would be remiss if I did not include a word concerning the central figure of the Christian faith, and what I view as his faith-lacking moment. Many who read this chapter may question my theology and down right disagree with me, but this account is in the Word for all to read, study, and learn from. So let's take a look at it.

Three of the four gospel writers record this exceptional moment in the life of Jesus; however, I would like to focus your attention to the gospel according to Luke, chapter 22, verses 39 through 46. There we will find Jesus heading to the Mount of Olives, which is normally a place of solitude and quiet for him and the disciples. When they arrive he immediately tells the disciples,

"Pray that you may not enter into temptation." He then walks "a stones throw" away and kneels to pray himself, but the words that he prays may catch you by surprise. He prays,

> *"Father, if it is Your will, take this cup away from me; nevertheless not my will, but Yours, be done."* (Luke 22:42)

For fear that you did not catch what was said, let me translate that.

> *Hey Dad, look man, I know You said I have to die for them, but can't You get one of the angels to do this instead of me; if I have to I will, but if I don't have to..*

Let me give you another one, in case you missed it.

> *Yo Pops, it's getting kind of close to that time, and I don't know about this cross thing. Can't You just wave Your hand and let me come home? I know we had a plan, but I thought I would offer You options.*

In my day, somebody close by, and overhearing these words, might start to cluck like a chicken. In this day and time, in this hip-hop culture, someone might issue a challenge to the Savior's claim to be the son of God. But, it's there in black and white and red. The Bible records it and it's in red, so Jesus said it. So let's investigate this a little further. The first question is, "Why did he say it?" The second question you might want to ask is, "What happened after he said it?

Why Did Jesus Pray What He Prayed?

Well, let me say this first, Jesus knew what his destiny was. It was to die on the cross to redeem man. Jesus said himself, in Luke 9, verse 22, *"The son of man must suffer many things, and be rejected by the elders, and chief priest, and scribes, and be killed, and be raised the third day."* In verse 42, the words that he prays seem to indicate a struggle with that destiny. Now, if this was anybody but Jesus, you would beat me to the punch line and say that the reason he said what he said was because he-lacked-the-faith-he-needed. You would say, like Moses, Jesus was trying to find a way out of, or around, his responsibility. You would say, like Esther, he thought he would escape because of his royalty. You would say, like Gideon, he was uncertain of who he was, who God was, and what God could do. You would say, like Joseph, he was trying to put this matter away privately. But, it is Jesus, and he is thinking "escapist" thoughts like Esther. It is Jesus, and he is having a Moses moment. It is Jesus, and he is uncertain like Gideon. It is Jesus, and he is looking for a loophole in the law to let him off the hook like Joseph. Yes, even Jesus had "a moment"; a moment when physical strength is low and

Yes, even Jesus had a moment.

emotional distress is high. A moment when his friends and comrades did not have his back. A moment when surroundings and happenings were taking their toll and messing with his soul. A moment when there was no resource that he could turn to but prayer, and so he prayed. He prayed honestly and he prayed openly. He prayed, *"Father, if it is Your will, take this cup away from me; nevertheless not my will, but Yours, be done."*

So now, what are you going to do with your theology? Don't answer that yet. Before you give me an answer, let's take a look at what happened after he prayed.

What Happened After Jesus Prayed?

After Jesus prayed, verse 43 says, *"Then an angel appeared to him from heaven, and strengthened him."* Yes, he looked no better than Esther, Gideon, Moses, Joseph, or you, when he said what he said. Nevertheless, it's what happened after he prayed that makes this moment significant to you and me. Because, even if we say he lacked the faith he needed, at least he did have sense enough to pray. But again, look what happened. His prayer was heard and answered. Some say, "God said, 'No.' " The text says, *"Then an angel appeared to him from heaven, and strengthened him."* When was "Then?"' After he prayed? So, I say his prayer was heard and answered.

But now, watch what happened. He prayed but, instead of letting him off the hook, God strengthened him. God, as the old folk would say, "propped him up on every leaning side." God, as the old folk would say, became his "leaning post." Isn't that what we really need when we are having a faith-lacking moment, strength?

Well, when you are struggling with your destiny and you lack the faith you need, pray, and God will strengthen you! Pray and God will strengthen you to stay in that marriage. Pray and God will strengthen you to stay in school. Pray and God will strengthen you to stay on that job. Pray and God will strengthen you to stay at your church. Pray and God will strengthen you to deal with those who persecute you. Pray and God will strengthen you!

Bibliography

CHAPTER 1

Chappell, Kevin. "*Serena As You've Never Seen Her Before*" Ebony. Oct. 2002: 164-165.

Dr. James & Shirley Dobson, *The Nightlight,* (Sisters, Oregon: Multnomah, 2000), 87.

CHAPTER 2

The Matrix, Warner Brothers, 2002. Dir.: Andy and Larry Wachowski. Perf.: Keanu Reeves, Lawrence Fishburn, Carry-Ann Moss.

Rev. Dr. Cameron M. Alexander, in a sermon at Antioch Baptist Church (Atlanta, GA.).

CHAPTER 5

Lockyer, Sr., Herbert with Bruce, F.F., and Harrison, R.F., *Illustrated Dictionary of the Bible*, (Nashville: Thomas Nelson Publishers, 1986) 1100.

Michael Jordan, *The Love of the Game,* (New York: Crown Publishers, 1999) 148.

CHAPTER 6

C*rimson Tide,* Hollywood Pictures, 1995. Director: Tony Scott. Perf.: Denzel Washington, Gene Hackman.

Earl "DMX" Simmons. "Who We Be" *The Great Depression,* Def Jam Records. 2001.

CHAPTER 7

A Civil Action, Touchstone, 1999. Dir.: Steven Zallian. Perf.: John Travolta, Robert Duvall.

An Officer and a Gentleman, Paramount Pictures, 1999. Director: Taylor Hackford. Performers: Richard Gere, Debra Winger, and Louis Gossett, Jr.

CHAPTER 8

Great is Thy Faithfulness. Thomas O. Chisholm, 1866-1960.

CHAPTER 9

Andy Young, *A Way Out of No Way: The Spiriitual Memoirs of Andy Young,* (Nashville: Nelson Publishers, 1994) 100-102.

Henry Blackaby, *Spiritual Leadership,* (Nashville: Broadman and Holman, 2001) 127.

Hayes, Ellen, "*Transformation of Robin Williams*" Reader's Digest Feb. 1999: 96-98.

About the Author

TONY A. MONTGOMERY, SR.
Pastor, Missionary Union Baptist Church

Reverend Tony A. Montgomery, Sr., is a native of Columbia, South Carolina. He is the son of Reverend and Mrs. James T. Montgomery (Pastor Emeritus of Temple Zion Baptist Church). He attended the public schools of Richland County and graduated from Lower Richland High School. Reverend Montgomery received a Bachelor of Arts degree with a major emphasis in Real Estate from Morehouse College in Atlanta, Georgia.

Following his graduation from Morehouse College, Rev. Montgomery spent several years working in the real estate appraisal profession and founded Atlanta Valuation Group, Inc., a commercial real estate appraisal and consulting firm in Atlanta. His dream was to eventually become a real estate developer; however, God's purpose was not that he build buildings, but rather develop Christians for Kingdom service.

Rev. Montgomery was licensed and ordained by the Antioch Baptist Church North in Atlanta, Georgia, and was an associate minister under the tutelage of Dr. Cameron M. Alexander for four years. At Antioch, Rev. Montgomery learned the art progressive leadership in the church and the community and added a great wealth of knowledge before being called to pastor Missionary Union Baptist Church in Columbus, MS, in 1996.

About the Author

Reverend Montgomery preaches a Christ-Centered, liberating gospel, and progressively leads Missionary Union in its mission to "manifest God's power by meeting the spiritual and physical needs of God's people." A believer in ministry that meets the spiritual and physical needs of God's people, Rev. Montgomery has led Missionary Union in developing various equipping and out-reach ministries; surrounding property has been acquired for expansion of the church campus; and a repair and restoration of the sanctuary was completed in 2001.

Reverend Montgomery's community service affiliations include former Member, Board of Directors, Columbus-Lowndes Economic Development Association; former Member, Board of Directors, Good Samaritan Free Medical Clinic; Member, Columbus-Lowndes County Inter-denominational Ministerial Alliance; Member, NAACP; former Member, Board of Directors, Columbus-Lowndes County Chamber of Commerce.

Reverend Montgomery is married to Attorney Monique Brooks-Montgomery of Columbus, Mississippi. They have three children, Sarah, Brooke, and Tony, II.